SAFE ZONE

TECHNOLOGICAL
ASPECTS OF
SAFETY IN THE WORKPLACE

By: Robert DuPrey Ph.D.

By: Robert DuPrey, Ph.D.

SAFE ZONE TECHNOLOGICAL ASPECTS OF SAFETY IN THE WORKPLACE

Cover design and illustration by Robert DuPrey

Order this book online at www.trafford.com
or email orders@trafford.com

Most Trafford titles are also available at major online book retailers.

Printed in Victoria, BC, Canada.

ISBN: 978-1-4269-2543-6

*Our mission is to efficiently provide the world's finest, most comprehensive book publishing
service, enabling every author to experience success. To find out how to publish your book, your
way, and have it available worldwide, visit us online at www.trafford.com*

Trafford rev. 01/20/2010

 www.trafford.com

North America & international
toll-free: 1 888 232 4444 (USA & Canada)
phone: 250 383 6864 ♦ fax: 812 355 4082

I dedicate this book to my best friend Harley

Robert DuPrey, Ph.D.

SAFE ZONE

Introduction

To succeed in workplace safety, organizations need good information, the ability to be a good leader, and the intelligence and inner strength to make good decisions regarding the safety of employees. Unfortunately, thousands of workers die each year, and many more suffer injury or illness from workplace conditions (Wardrop, 2001). An effective accident prevention program requires proper job performance from everyone in the workplace. The first step to organizing an outstanding workplace safety plan is to adopt a zero-accidents goal (Slaughter and Ghormley, 1991). History shows that poorly managed projects tend to have both poor productivity and safety, whereas better managed projects tend to have better productivity and safety Gibson, 1992). Greater emphasis should be placed on the early phases of safety project planning and development so that a safety project is not allowed to get out of control.

The purpose of this book is to analyze and contrast the research and literature on work place safety as it relates to incentives and employee attitudes. The writer will first define safety culture. Second, OSHA and the lack of safety issues will be discussed. Third, the leadership factors and safety training will be analyzed. Finally, the safety incentives and employee attitude toward safety in the workplace and a conclusion will be laid out.

Workplace Safety

As organizations move away from traditional and hierarchical management styles, a growing number of organizations are taking steps to involve the people at the sharp end of production in safety management. In light of the staggering numbers attributed to workplace injuries, organizations are recognizing the value associated with keeping the workplace safe. There is a link between workplace safety and a company's performance (Gregg, 2001). He identifies three benefits for improving workplace safety: reducing employee pain and suffering; avoiding the direct cost of workplace injuries; and preventing the indirect costs of these injuries, which include lower employee morale, lost productivity and the expense of hiring or training overtime (Gregg, 2001). Safety is not a luxury in the organizations, where safety programs are the first lines of defense against unnecessary loss of life, property, and injury.

Geller (1994) writes, "Behaviors which reduce the probability for injury often involve environment change and produce attitudes consistent with the safe behaviors, especially if these behaviors are viewed as voluntary" (pp. 29-34). In other words, when employees choose to act safely, they act themselves into safe thinking and such behaviors often result in some environmental change.

A safety research study by Jannadi and Assaf (1994) have revealed that safety level in job sites varies with the project size. Large projects, they say, have a better average safety level than small projects. They also concluded that the safety level is mainly related to the type of the project. Johnson (1988) writes, "Management accountability must be directed toward loss prevention rather than loss reduction ... this accountability could be measured with safety audits, inspection results, safety sampling, developing of accident reduction goals and safety performance reviews" (pp. 23-26).

Safety Culture

Safety culture in organizations should be created to encourage employees at all levels. It is organizational culture that encourages all employees to proactively search their work areas for hazards, admonish co-workers who are doing things unsafely, and communicate to peers and superiors about matters that affect safety (Covaleski, 1996). The basic building block for workplace safety cultures are behavior modification programs that provide consistent positive reinforcement to workers who voluntarily act to improve safety on the job (Palcznski, 1992). The advocates, such as Peterson (1995), say "These cultures represent the latest gradation in corporate America's ever-increasing awareness of safety as a major factor in bottom-line costs" (p. 28).

Geller (1995) writes, "Safety coaching is a key process in developing a total safety culture ... the more employees that effectively apply safety coaching principles, the closer an organization will be to achieving total safety culture" (pp. 16-22). McCann (2000) writes, Safety cultures represent the next level because, by encouraging all employees to take responsibility for safety, they transcend what has been workers' all-too-typical attitude of merely looking for someone else to blame when an accident occurs ... most companies already have good records on safety, but they want to push up to the next level.

Employers may use different means to develop a workplace safety culture, but all the cultures have the same goal to motivate all workers to be proactive and positive factors in improving workplace safety. Business managers call this "empowering" employee. Empowering employees can be done by making all employees part of the company safety committee (Salmans, 2000). The idea is to make everyone part of the safety process as opposed to creating a safety team responsible for looking over people's shoulders.

Mattila, Rentanen and Hyttinen (1994) conducted a safety research study to determine whether there is any connection between the quality of the work environment and occupational safety. Their study proved that the quality of the work environment and the level of safety are directly connected and the high quality work environment will improve the housekeeping and reduce the accident frequency rates. Shields (1994) writes, "Effective human relations skills will help supervisors promote and improve safety by developing a climate of teamwork" (pp. 40-42). Human relations skills are key in any organization because people are the ones performing the work. Safety management, which effectively uses such skills to improve employee management relations, will achieve the desired safety goals. Glen (2001) writes, The workplace safety culture concept in some respects is a byproduct of the Total Quality Management (TQM) movement that began in the 1980s ... by regularly and systematically addressing safety, and providing a format in which safe practices are recognized, the teams seek to make the TQM mantra, constant and never-ending improvement, part of company safety.

A key component of TQM systems at many businesses is a quality team that convenes regularly to discuss and map quality strategies in an effort to create a better safety environment (Lasey, 1994, p. 27). The Total Quality Management (TQM) philosophy argues quality strategies that include safety should be done with input from people throughout the organization, especially frontline workers, and from the customers and clients the organization serves (Miller, 1992).

Within our organization, we've done all things necessary to be in compliance with prescribed safety standards, but that is not enough (Feeney, 2000). Feeney (2000) continues that this safety culture is the way to provide continuous improvement.

Occupational Safety and Health

Administration

The reality of the hazards inherent in organizations has resulted in the creation of government and industry regulations and operating procedures that contribute to reducing accidents and injury. Kibert and Coble (1995) write, "Integrating safety environmental regulation would provide a single agency that would eliminate conflicts, duplication of regulations and information, and increase efficiency and quality of worker safety and environmental protection" (pp. 95-99).

Barr (2001) writes, "The government stepped in with Occupational Safety and Health Administration (OSHA) and put together the rules and regulations because the employers had not done enough" (p. 4). He continues, "Since then, employers have recognized that workers were injured because of the lack of safety procedures and that meant less money for the company ... they began focusing on safety independent of regulations" (p. 4). OSHA regulations cover areas such as: establishing safety standards, conducting safety inspections, granting safety variances for organizations that are unable to comply with standards and citing organizations where standards are being violated. The Occupational Safety and Health Administration (OSHA) Act of 1970 is the preeminent federal law governing workplace safety and health in the United States (Robinowitz and Hager, 2000). OSHA, which is situated within the Department of Labor, "holds primary policy-making and enforcement responsibility" (Martin and Wogalter, 1991, pp. 931-935). OSHA funds education and training efforts and state consultation programs, monitors state OSHA performance, and coordinates voluntary compliance initiatives.

"The National Institute for Occupational Safety and Health (NIOSH), a division of the Centers for Disease Control within the Department of Health and Human Services, is OSHA's research partner" (U.S.C. sections 669(e)). NIOSH develops non-binding scientific criteria and recommendations for OSHA's use in standard-setting, conducts health hazard evaluations, and provides technical assistance to labor, management, and other government agencies (Hager, 2000).

The negative aspect of OSHA is the complexity of it. Very few U.S. companies meet all OSHA regulations ... the number and complexity of regulations makes it difficult to comply with every requirement (Jones, 1999). Although most standards mandate that firms maintain records, record keeping also is a requirement in itself.

Critics claim that over time OSHA has become an unwieldy bureaucracy, more intent on paperwork and government rules than on safety and health (Ballenger, 1995), and that it has moved from its original purpose of protecting workers to hindering business with excessive mandates (Gregg, 2001). Businesses decry OSHA's unwieldy, difficult, and sometimes inconsistent 4,000-plus regulations claiming that 50 percent of inspectors' violations are for incorrectly written forms (Howard, 1994). OSHA was not created to be the friend of employers ... it's to protect American workers from serious hazards through promulgation of effective standards and strong enforcement of the law (O'Neill, 1995).

Lack of Safety

There are many reasons for lack of safety in the workplace. Hoffman and Stetzer (1996) list, "pressure to complete work quickly, inadequate organizational procedures for routine hazards, ineffective communication on safety and a focus on production as opposed to safety at the management level" (p. 84). They suggest, "Work pressure may lead to perceptions that short cuts are necessary to meet demands" (p. 84). Lack of communication may set norms that discourage approaching others engaged in unsafe behavior.

Other factors might include "the degree of emphasis on production rather than safety ... the development of work plans with not enough time to allow for safe performance" (Everett & Adelhamid, 2000, p. 52). In some cases, the actions of management set a "safety climate for the organization" (Boggs, 1995, p. 38). Kovach and Hamilton (1997) write, "Workers perception of management commitment to safety such as training programs, management participation in safety committees, review of work pace, and consideration of safety in job design, was related to both frequency of unsafe acts and accidents" (p. 57).

On an average day, 14 people are killed and more than 10,400 are disabled on the job — a death toll equivalent to a major airline disaster every two weeks ... less visible are the estimated 60,000 deaths caused each year by job-related illnesses ... the cost to the economy of workplace injuries exceeds $127 billion a year — more than the combined profits of the 17 most profitable U.S. corporations (Safety Research report, 2000).

According to Hoffmann and Stetzer (1996), "Safety interventions tend to focus on the individual to the neglect of broader factors that may implicitly reward unsafe behavior" (p. 84). They indicate, "Safety practitioners should consider organizational diagnosis to identify root causes of unsafe behavior and accidents" (p. 84). Swift (2001) writes, "The workplace has been identified as the greatest single source of stress" (p. 6). The causes of such stress can range from the anxieties produced by corporate downsizing to factors that result in physical disorders.

In the 1990s, the introduction of personal computer systems changed the workplace. Virtually every worker has a computer on his or her desk. Healy (2001) writes, "Problems that traditionally plagued typists, such as carpal tunnel syndrome, now are more common" (p. 48). People are spending more time at work than ever before, which could be a factor contributing to the alarming increase in unsafe acts both personal and work related. However, just as these problems arise in the workplace, so do ways to identify and correct them.

Arkin (1996) writes, "The majority of workplace safety programs have concentrated on improving control systems without looking into the behaviors of workers ... given that people can be potentially dangerous even to themselves" (p. 37). He adds, "Behavioral methods should be employed to minimize worker behaviors that lead to accidents and injuries in the workplace" (p. 37).

Leadership Factor

Dial (1992) writes, "Total management commitment and total management involvement in safety is the major controlling influence in obtaining success" (pp. 37-45). No endeavor within an organization can function effectively without strong support from top management. For safety to be an effective program there must be a commitment at the highest level in the organization. The commitment must include a clear statement that safety is important and support for actions that will make safety important (Brauer, 1990).

Duff, Robertson, Phillips and Cooper (1994) conducted a safety study in the development and effects of behaviorally based management techniques in improving safety. The results of their study show that safety behavior can be objectively and reliably measured without excessive use of managerial or supervisory resources, and producing performance data that can be used in many different safety management strategies, which will produce large improvements in safety performance. Their study also shows that the commitment of management appears to enhance the effectiveness of the goal setting and feedback approach.

Managerial commitment is a key factor in a training program, there is a direct correlation between good management and a good safety record (Hammer, 1989). A strong commitment is manifested by active leadership, sustained interest, total support, participation and the delegation of responsibility with accountability (Jackson, 1981). To achieve a safer workplace, the executives and managers are required to create safety values. The leadership factor in creating values, company directions, performance expectations, customer loyalty and stakeholder focus in the same manner that learning and innovation factors are all important to quality (Warrack, 1999).

Harner (1983) writes, "Commitment without [management] involvement is meaningless ... good attitude is related to and depends upon the involved commitment of management" (pp. 13-15). Heinrich (1959) has studied the contribution of both unsafe acts and unsafe conditions. He analyzed 75,000 accidents and found that 88 percent were caused by unsafe acts or unsafe operation, 10 percent from unsafe conditions or unsafe work locations, and 2 percent from unpreventable causes.

Pancucci (1990) writes, "A leader walks the walks and talks the talk" (p. 30). Leaders set a personal example in many ways by wearing protective equipment, participating on their firms safety committee, and committing the resources needed if and when required to make safety improvements. In a safety research study by Manitoba (1998), he found that when managers and workers were asked to rank the importance of four factors: quality, safety, costs and productivity, both employers and workers ranked "safety" first, and both groups ranked "quality" as the second priority. "Costs and productivity and production" were ranked at third and fourth places respectively. This type of leadership belief, that safety is the number one corporate priority, helps to set the better safety performers apart from poor performers.

Senior managers are required to guide the company in setting the overall workplace safety objectives and to sustain their safety-related leadership in all activities associated with safety at the same level as quality. Managers must communicate safety's number one priority in relation to the corporate values, strategic plans, performance expectations and organizational learning in order to use their knowledge base to continuously make refinements in improved safety performance policies (Dunlop, 1994). He continues that safety performance must remain an area of regular reviews and audits to ensure that continuous improvement occurs in goals and objectives.

Based on safety research done by researchers such as Thompson (1991), Jenkins (1990), Kimmerling (1985) and Rothwell (1989), the following characteristics of an effective safety management program were defined as: "1) top management support and reinforcement of safety standards" (Thompson, 1991, pp. 45-53); "2) employee involvement in suggesting safer work procedures and the selection of equipment (Jenkins, 1990, pp. 54-56); "3) regular and recurring safety training programs that reinforce safety standards and behaviors" (Rothwell, 1989, pp. 53-54); and "4) effective monitoring systems to ensure standards and behaviors being practiced and to correct and unsafe conditions" (Kimmerling, 1985, pp. 50-55).

Regardless of the size of an organization, leaders, managers and employees should use safety standards and safety procedures to prevent workplace accidents and possible injuries and illnesses. Developing workplace safety programs should lead organizations to do all the things needed to protect employees in job safety. An organization's attitude towards job safety will be reflected by the organization's employees (Glen, 2000). If an organization is not interested in preventing employee injury and illness, nobody else is likely to be. Leaders should demonstrate their concern for employee safety and health in the workplace at all times. Meyer and Allen (1998) write, "An organization's policy must be clearly set to demonstrate the depth of its commitment by involving employees in planning and carrying out its efforts" (p. 245).

Safety Training

A training program backed with strong commitment by management will be successful and will aid in decreasing accident rates (Chissick and Derricott, 1981). Researchers are discovering that skills training, aimed at increasing workplace safety and productivity, also may increase personal safety off the job. Many of the programs and training sessions designed to increase safety and productivity on the job also provide employees with enhanced life skills (Wilmot, 2000). The development of a safety training program should include research findings regarding effective presentation of safety information (Roland and Moriarty, 1990). In searching for the best method to increase compliance with safety information and risk perception, researchers have focused primarily on the presentation of hazard information. According to Martin and Wogalter (1991), "Hazard information has been presented by exhibiting the severity of injury by accident scenarios by stating the consequences of non-compliance in order to lead to increased risk perception" (pp. 931-935).

Creating a safe work environment goes beyond traditional workplace hazard training and includes concerns about individual safety. Sanders and McCormick (1993) write, "The perceived risk or hazard associated with a situation influences worker behavior and the degree that the worker takes precautionary actions to prevent injuries" (pp. 675-677). Many researchers such as Wilde (1982) have found that "perceived risk is based upon an individual's past experience, the perceived potential for an unsafe incident, and an individuals' assessment of his/her own ability to cope physically and mentally with a hazardous situation" (pp. 209-225). Wogalter (1991) writes, "The principle component of risk perception is injury severity" (pp. 133-140).

During 1980-1996, research findings indicated that training creates safer workplaces through increased worker knowledge of job hazards and safe work practices in a wide array of workplaces (Smith & Berenger, 1989, pp. 767-789). Safety training programs are an important factor in organizations. Is it estimated that 68 percent of organizations conduct some form of safety training (Industry Report, 1996).

Dear (1995) writes, "To achieve safety goals, the strategies must address workplace safety, training employers to take an active role in administering their programs, early intervention in work-related illnesses and injuries, greater emphasis on managed care and personal contact with injured workers" (p. 39). Personnel education and training on safety have been identified as administrative solutions to minimize the exposure of workers to occupational hazards.

The purpose of safety education and training is to ensure that employees are sufficiently informed about the hazards they may be exposed to and therefore be able to apply correct procedures to avoid them (Chissick and Derricott, 1981).

Safety Incentives and Employee Attitude

One of the factors that may be used to motivate employees in workplace safety is quality award and incentive criteria. Pelletier (1993) views "incentive systems as motivation tools" (pp. 4-6). Giustina and Danier (1989) conducted a safety research study on quality of work life through employee motivation. The findings of their study illustrated three contributions management can offer employees to improve safety in the workplace: "1) knowledge and understanding of safe work practices, 2) a strongly shared belief that top management is truly committed to safety and health, and 3) management's recognition and support for changes in work behavior to achieve the desired safe work behaviors that will stimulate workers to take responsibility for change" (pp. 24-28).

Active employee safety participation produces a sense of belonging. Eckhardt (1993) writes, "The workforce develops an internal motivation ... this involvement results in higher moral and improved work performance which impacts growth and success" (pp. 16-20).

Attitude is the worker's feeling of favorableness or feeling unfavorable toward performing a behavior (Gordon, 1994). Positive attitude toward safety procedures in organizations can be explained as how well safety professionals meet safety responsibilities. Accidents will decrease when attitude improves as a result of performing safety procedures. According to a safety research study by Gallagher (1993), "As a positive attitude toward safety increased, the number of accidents per worker dramatically decreased" (pp. 29-33).

Hidley and Krause (1994) write, "Managing safety for

continuous improvement requires a behavior-based performance, rather than attitude-based" (pp. 28-32). Hinze, Bern and Piepho (1995) conducted a safety study of the importance of experience modification rating as a measure of safety performance. They have concluded, "The safety modifier is an incentive for the organizations to strive for good safety records" (pp. 455-458). They have found that the organization with poor safety records will pay higher premiums. Their findings suggested that the experience modification rating is not an appropriate measure of safety performance for all companies.

Lateiner (1969) conducted a safety research study of the importance of attitude in controlling incidents and improving safety performance. Through a survey for supervisors of 47 companies, he found that as a positive attitude toward safety increased, the number of accidents per employee dramatically decreased. He concluded that the development of a sound safety attitude throughout an enterprise was predicted on how well supervisors met safety responsibilities. Mattila (1994) writes, "Accidents will decrease when attitudes improve as a result of supervisors effectively performing safety procedures" (pp. 257-268).

Topf and Petrino (1995) write, "The development of safe attitudes is the key to promoting safe behavior ... positive attitudes toward safety will encourage the employees to discuss safety issues and concerns without waiting for supervisor to do so" (pp. 24-27). Such proactive behavior occurs when employees are keyed into preventive safety efforts. Without attitudinal changes and a strong sense of personal accountability, employees will not take responsibility for safety. Instead, they will revert to unsafe behavior or inaction once the observer is removed.

Some safety motivational tools such as safety

incentives are being used in many organizations. According to McGill (1989), "Some of the incentive programs are: salary increases, fringe benefits, morale boosters and management by objectives" (pp. 181-187). McGill (1989) adds that "salary increases are of two types: across-the-board cost of living raises and merit increases" (pp. 181-187). Merit increases given to employees for a job well done, if given to a small number of employees, serve as a motivator. Fringe benefits and morale boosters such as insurance and paid vacation when paired with adequate salary is more favored by employees (McGill, 1989). Reward system provides evidence that safety award criteria can be used not just as a basis to assess safety and health performance issues, but that its concepts and principles can be tailored to meet all workplaces' safety requirements and their successes in driving similar strategies and action plans (Warrack and Sinha, 1999).

Rewards for outstanding safety performance should not be different from those given for quality achievement, so after responsibilities are established and objectives are set, the only way to achieve them is to hold the person accountable. People are motivated through incentives and rewards. Eckhardt (1993) writes, "The use of safety incentive plans must avoid using competition between crews, which may pressure workers and encourage them to take unsafe short cuts" (pp. 16-20).

It is important to design a pay incentive plan that not only rewards people for effective effort but also keeps them motivated to do better and grow with the company. In many cases, many companies are using safety award programs as a tool for raising the employee's awareness of safety and offering him/her a tangible incentive to perform his/her job in a safe fashion. Sheridan (1992) writes, "Workers can earn points in purchasing gifts from a catalog if safety is maintained is a certain level" (pp. 74-76).

Buckman (1991) states, "Strategies that can help companies motivate, reward, and retain valuable employees focus on intrinsic rewards ... compensation, benefits, bonuses, and perquisites rewards are secondary" (p. 19).

Changing a person's attitude can effectively be accomplished by making a change in his/her belief system. Therefore, a worker's beliefs about safety hazards determine his/her attitude about using safe equipment to protect him/herself. In a research by Goldhaber and deTurck (1988) the authors stated, "Significant variations in risk perception have been shown between gender and age group demographics" (pp. 29-37). Many gender differences are found in the literature that females are more likely to act safely, and intentionally look for and read safety warnings. Young (1989) has found in his research that "females read warning messages on labels of potentially hazardous products" and it has been shown that "females rate products as significantly more hazardous than males" (pp. 503-507). Results of a study by Braun (1995) revealed, "Safety hazards were better understood by the user when consequence information was a component" (pp. 346-350). Dejoy (1989) reported, "Strong and consistent data exist to show that people who feel threatened by potential serious injury will be more likely to comply with safety warning information" (pp. 936-939). Familiarity has also been shown to be a factor in risk perception (Godfrey, 1983, pp. 950-954). Slovic (1978) states that "risk will be more acceptable and the product or task is perceived as less hazardous if the situation is familiar to the user" (pp. 58-68).

Technological Aspects

New technology has changed the U.S. economy's mix of jobs and industries. Computers have revolutionized work and workplaces and raised the skill requirements for many jobs. Demand for higher-skilled leaders has become increasingly important. Where strength and manual dexterity used to be enough to ensure employment and a comfortable standard of living, more jobs now and in the future will require verbal and mathematical skills, as well as leadership in organizational and interpersonal skills. Drucker (1999) writes, "Skills will need updating as technology introduces new ways of completing age-old tasks" (p. 73).

The purpose of this paper is to synthesize how

technology and effective leadership can contribute to the success of an organization. The writer will analyze and evaluate the themes that will be most significant in the next decade. This paper first reviews the technology and the leadership elements separately. The remaining actions will be the future of technology and leadership.

Technology

Technology has changed organization's perception of reality. As a result of the changes in technology, the industry is converging on a new computing model that enables a standard way of building business applications to connect and exchange information over the Web (Gates, 2001). Technology also has changed the productive forces, economic structure and ideological culture of the western society. Technology inserts data in between the worker and the product (Zuboff, 1988). Drucker (1999) writes, "The factory worker no longer manipulates the sheet of steel, instead they manipulate the data about the steel" (p. 73).

Advances in the computer industry, coupled with those in telecommunications, have created the new information technology. A report by the U.S. Department of Commerce projections (1999) shows that by 2006, nearly half of all U.S. workers will be employed in industries that produce or intensively use information technology, products, and services.

The impact of these technological changes has been so pervasive, and so dramatic in size and speed that is has been difficult to describe. According to Information Week (2001), "Starting in the 1950s, an entirely new industry was established, led by the large mainframe computer companies such as IBM, RCA, Honeywell, and Univac ... these companies opened a host of new jobs producing, maintaining, and servicing computer systems" (p. 30). The life span of a personal computer provides one illustration of the diminishing time between introduction and obsolescence of new technologies. USA Today (1999) reports "The average life of a personal computer, or PC, has decreased from 4 1/2 years in 1992 to just over 3 years

in 1999, and is predicted to be only 2 years by 2007" (p.

3A). To understand the dynamics of the transformation

underway, it is important to grasp both the scope and the

speed of this revolution. Drucker (1999) writes, Beginning

with the widespread introduction of large mainframe

computers in the 1950s and '60s, followed by steady

advances in computing power that permitted a decrease in

their physical size ... the introduction and dramatic growth

of personal computers in the 1980s took even the computer

industry by surprise, threatening the mainframe operations

of the larger companies ... computers moved into millions

of American homes. (p. 102)

Herman (1999) writes, "The computer and

information technology revolutions have changed virtually

every industry in the economy ... new jobs have been

created in airfreight and delivery systems to service such

just-in-time inventory operations ... handheld mobile phones have become commonplace, and digital phone systems will soon be able to reach anyone in the world via satellite" (p. 209). The technological revolution has also launched entirely new industries. Literally hundreds of new companies have emerged in areas unheard of a decade ago. Cranch (1991) writes, "Technology and job creations are linked together" (pp. 237-252). Judy and D'Amico (1997) write, Computer-manufacturing jobs skyrocketed until 1984 as American producers dominated world production of all kinds of computers ... between the appearance of the first PCs in the mid-1970s and 1983, computer industry jobs in the United States grew by nearly 80 percent, while total U.S. manufacturing employment grew by only 4 percent". (p. 17)

Most leaders and workers will need basic computer skills to enter their chosen occupations and additional specialized training in field-specific applications to advance.

High technology has added over one million jobs to the U.S. economy since 1993 (Platzer, 1999). It will indeed be a world that rewards lifelong learning. Barley (1999) mentions, "with all these influences on business practices ... the need for knowledge has become vital" (p. 7). Meister (1994) writes, "It is a process where all levels of employees, as well as key customers and suppliers, are involved in continuous lifelong learning to improve their performance on the job" (p. 30).

According to Atkinson and Court (1998) "virtually all of the jobs that were lost in goods production and distribution since 1969 have been offset by office jobs and computers" (p.9). Rather than industrial machinery, tools such as telephones, fax machines, and personal computers are utilized in organizations. With the rapid introduction of mobile phones, laptops, e-mail, and the Internet, the traditional time and space requirements of workers are no longer the rigid constraints of the past. In particular, the growth in computer applications and the Internet has enormous potential to help lower barriers to job opportunity for workers with disabilities.

Rifkin (1995) writes, "The effect of technological change is amplified by the very strategies that organizations currently use to cope with the change … because leaders have to make decisions more quickly, organizations are shortening their chains of command, flattening their hierarchies, and handing the authority for many decisions to frontline employees" (p. 17). Because organizations and leaders want to speed up production of goods and delivery of services, they turn over the redesign of their processes to cross-trained and self-managing teams of technology experts. This changes not only what is done but also who has the power to determine what will be done.

Bridges (1994) writes "Technology renders jobs obsolete by replacing the relatively slowly changing world of things with the much more mercurial world of data" (p. 14). The new information and communication technologies have increased the volume and accelerated the flow of activity at every level of society. According to Loveman and Chris (1988), "The restructuring of the corporation is fast eliminating middle management from the organizational chart" (pp. 46-65). They point out "while better jobs are being created for a fortunate few at the top levels of management, the men and woman in garden variety middle management jobs are getting crucified by corporate re-engineering and the introduction of sophisticated new information and communication technologies" (pp. 46-65). A growing number of companies are deconstructing their organizational hierarchies by compressing several jobs into a single process. They are then using the computer to perform the coordination functions previously carried out by many people often working in separate departments and locations within the company.

Authors Davidow and Malone (1992) note, "Computers can gather most information more accurately and cost effectively than people. They can produce summaries with electronic speeds and they can transmit the information to decision-makers at the speed of light" (p. 126). They continue by saying, "Most interesting is that frequently this information is so good and the analysis so precise that an executive decision is no longer required" (p. 126). A well-trained employee dealing directly with the situation can now make the decision faster and in a more responsive fashion than the remote manager can miles away.

Organizations are rapidly shifting from an economy based on manufacturing and commodities to one that places the greatest value on information, services, support, and distribution ... that shift, in turn, places an unprecedented premium on knowledge workers, a new class of affluent, educated, and mobile people who view themselves as free agents in a seller's market (Noriha and Goshal, 1997). Knowledge workers and leaders with the latest technology will create speedy business processes in organizations. This technological speed is quickly becoming a critical success factor. Spencer (1998) writes "Virtually every industry has seen vast changes in the way it designs, produces, or reaches the market with its offerings" (p. 34). Rifkin (1995) mentions, "The rash of current technological breakthroughs and economic restructuring initiatives seem to have descended on workers with little warning" (p.101).

While the new information technology and robotics are changing the nature of some industries, management has been replacing machines for human labor in virtually

every area of activity. Skills will need updating as
technology introduces new ways of completing age-old
tasks. Leontief (1982) believes, Technological change is
inevitable; they admit that the emerging knowledge sector
will not be able to create enough jobs to absorb the millions
of workers displaced by re-engineering and automation (...)
favors a shortening of the workweek as a means of sharing
the available work. (pp. 194-195)

The constructive use of leisure, he further argues,
"can come about only with an improvement in education"
(p. 194). Organizational learning, which leads to corporate
growth, is achieved through individual development (Senge,
1990). Swanson and Torraco (1995) write, "Training is for
the good of plant production, it is a way to solve
production problems through people, it is specific and
helps people to acquire skills through the use of what thy
learned" (p. 2).

Technology Problems

Technology has helped to create a highly complex world with numerous new problems - problems that were once either nonexistent or insoluble. In using technology to resolve the problems, organizations are creating whole new sets of problems. Watkins (1996) writes, "Industrialization resolved for many people the problem of survival ... it has revived the problem in terms of the pollution of the environment" (pp. 89-96)). Mills (1999) writes, "When technological changes are instituted that increase the efficiency of output, but decrease human relations in groups, employees will resist the change ... managers often become overly motivated about a technological change that will bring increased organizational recognition and rewards" (p. 34). With an increasing number of workers being displaced by new labor saving technologies and with production soaring, the business community desperately searched for new ways to reorient the psychology of existing wage earners, to draw them into what Cowdrick (1927) calls "the new economic gospel of consumption" (p.208). The new high technology revolution could mean fewer hours of work.

Non-traditional workers receive fewer benefits, such as health care, vacation, unemployment compensation, or pensions, than do full-time workers (DeSimone and Harris, 1998). This raises challenges for corporations on a number of fronts.

Drucker (1999) writes, "Unemployment is a major risk factor" (p. 73). In the information age, more sophisticated software technologies are bringing civilization ever closer to a near workless world.

High-tech stress for both machinery and employees
causes organizations millions of dollars. According to a
study conducted by the National Institute of Occupational
Safety and Health (NIOSH), "clerical workers who use
computers suffer inordinately high levels of stress" (cited in
Brod, 1984). High stress levels often lead to health related
problems. Rifkin (1995) writes, "The new computer-based
technologies have so quickened the volume, flow, and pace
of information that millions of workers are experiencing
mental overload and burnout" (p. 188). Stress on the
computer systems is also causing problems for
organizations. According to Parker and Slaughter (1988),
"Stressing the system can be accomplished by increasing
the line sped, cutting the number of people or machines, or
giving workers more tasks ... a line can be balanced by
decreasing resources or increasing the work load at
positions that always run smoothly ... once problems have

been corrected, the system can be further stressed" (p. 37).

Another critical factor in utilizing technology in the workplace is that the productivity has shifted from physical to mental response. Rifkin (1995) writes, "Companies are continually experimenting with new methods to optimize the interface between employees and their computers ... visual display units are being programmed so that if the operator does not respond to the data on the screen within seventeen seconds it disappears" (p. 188). These sorts of operation may cause employees a high level of stress; even small subtle changes in the office routine may increase the stress level of workers.

Leadership

Jago (1982) defines leadership as "the use of noncoercive influence to direct and coordinate the activities of a group toward accomplishing a goal" (p. 47). Leadership is a complex subject that has been approached in a number of different ways. Pfeffer (1977) writes, "While there have been many studies of leadership, the dimension and definition of the concept remain unclear" (p. 104). Leadership is one of the most extensive researched constructs in the behavioral sciences (Stogdill, 1981). Early theories of leadership tended to explain leadership effectiveness in terms of the leader. Many theories focused on the qualities of the individuals and how those qualities influenced the individual's effectiveness. White and Bednar (1986) state, "The 'Greatman' leadership theory suggested that great leaders were born, not made" (p. 491). They continue by saying, "Such men and women were believed to possess certain qualities that lead them to greatness" (p. 491).

According to Fiedler (1967), "A leader can be effective only if his or her personal style is appropriately matched to a given set of situational variables" (p. 149). Perhaps one of the best examples of this personal style is the leadership of Mahatma Gandhi, who claimed that his life was my own message. He said, "You must watch my life, how I live, eat, sit, talk, and behave in general. The sum total of all those is my religion" (quoted in Nair, 1994). Gandhi believed that his personal life gave him the credibility that enabled him to be a successful leader.

Fiedler believes that each person has a particular leadership style, based on his or her needs, that dictates how he or she will act. Fiedler (1967) states the problem with this kind of leadership model is that since "this style is based on the leader's needs, it is very difficult for the leader to change it" (p. 190). According to Fiedler (1964), "Personal style of leadership will not be effective in all situations ... it is therefore the leader's task to diagnose the situation and either place himself in a situation favorable to his style or modify the situation so that it becomes favorable to his style" (p. 189).

Regarding other theories of leadership, White and Bednar (1986) mention, "the trait approach attempted to identify specific traits and characteristics that leaders held in common" (p. 491). The qualities, characteristics, and skills required in a leader are determined to a large extent by the demands of the situation in which he is to function as a leader (Stogdill, 1981). There are, however, some positive and negative traits that leaders may also hold. The positive characteristics of leadership are enthusiasm, risk taking, fairness and an unquestioned career ethic (McGregor, 1978). Some of the negative characteristics of leadership are manipulation, seduction, and the perpetual adolescent need for adventure that are causing distrust and unnecessary crises (McGregor, 1978). But unless leaders' negative traits are transformed or controlled, even most gifted leaders become liabilities as leaders in a new economic reality.

All of the leadership theories identify one central component of the complex human situation. Some the theories lack a concern with organizational dynamics. Hesselbein, Goldsmith and Beckhard (1996) write, "Organizations have different needs and problems at different stages in their evolution ... we tend to tread the topic of leadership in a vacuum instead of specifying what the leader's relationship to the organization is at any given time" (p. 60). The relationship between the leader and the organization becomes complex at times, so a beginning leadership model for analysis should be useful. Some leadership styles like Peters (1984) focuses on "getting things done, keeping up with the information and innovation in the organization, hierarchy-less organizations, outsmarting global competitors, breaking the mold, developing professional networks, and leading change, not following it" (p. 5). Leadership style focuses on inspiring people at every level of an organization. Blanchard (1993) notes that it is essential to create mutual respect and enthusiastic teamwork in the workplace. By doing so, Blanchard (1993) asserts that same consideration and efficiency naturally extends to the people responsible for any company's survival.

Based on White and Bednar's (1986) conclusion, "Some people may think they will be effective leaders because they have certain family ties or possess certain traits" (p. 493). Atkerson (1976) writes, "No evidence exits that either family background or a limited number of personal characteristics will consistently contribute to an individual's ability to lead" (p. 9). What is important is the leadership style and the way he or she can operate. House (1971) mentions that there are four styles of leadership: "directive, supportive, participative and achievement-oriented" (p. 321).

Directive Leadership

Directive leadership style focuses on specific directions given to subordinates. House (1971) writes, "A leader tells subordinates what is expected of them and gives specific directions ... a leader may answer questions; however, a leader does not solicit subordinate suggestions" (p. 329). In this style the path for success will be led by the leader.

Supportive Leadership

Supportive leadership emphasizes work-group needs and subordinates' well being. House (1971) writes, "A leader is open and shows a genuine concern for subordinates' wellbeing and comfort ... a leader tries to create a friendly climate and to satisfy team needs" (p. 329). In this style of leadership the support for the group and team dynamics should be taken into account and to ensure what is given to the group is transferred back to the job. It is clear that high performing teams are the most important business trend for the future (Blanchard, 1993). In this style of leadership, the leader and subordinates tread each other as customers (internal). The need to delight customers (internal and external) in terms of quality, cost, and service is not a one-time effort ... to get and retain customers (internal and external) companies must consistently attempt

to improve upon their basic competitive practices

(Blanchard, 1993)

Participative Leadership

Participative leadership style works on a leader's participation and asks for feedback from subordinates. House (1971) writes, "A leader asks subordinates for information and encourages them to share their ideas ... the leader considers inputs but still makes the decision" (p. 320). Managers can benefit from a multifaceted channel of communication and feedback by being a good listener, communicating openly and handling differences of opinion constructively (Lawler, 1992).

Achievement-Oriented Leadership

In this leadership style, the leader is goal oriented and works with the team to achieve them. House (1971) writes, "A leader sets results-oriented, challenging goals and expresses confidence in the subordinates' ability to achieve them ... responsibility for goal attainment rests with subordinates" (p. 329). DeSimone and Harris (1998) concluded, "Research convincingly shows that goals that are specific, difficult and accepted by leaders will lead to higher levels of performance than easy, vague goals or no goals at all" (p. 36). Blanchard (1993) emphasizes on teamwork and group development. He argues that teamwork is essential for anyone who works with groups and wants to build a high performing team.

Other leadership models such as Situational Leadership was first developed by Blanchard. The situational leadership concept provides the typology linking organizational power bases, workforce maturity, and leadership style. The result of a research study by Avery (1985) reveals that in the situational leadership the power bases perceived by the executives and their subordinates are generally different. Avery (1985) finds that the subordinate's perception of the executive power bases were more closely related to selling and participating leadership styles.

Many other leadership theories are based on support, task performance and goal attainment. White and Bednar (1986) write, "Researchers have identified two primary dimensions of leadership: 1) the psychological support and concern shown for employees and 2) the attention given to task performance and goal attainment" (p. 513). Other theorists believe that leaders of today's organizations should build trust and empower employees on their job responsibilities.

Kotter (1996) writes, "Leadership operates in a trust-based environment ... employees are empowered by trust and given the freedom to fulfill their job responsibilities" (p. 161). People are important and they come first before goals and visions. Peters (1987) argues, "The vision is what the organization should try to achieve" (p. 482). Peters (1987) writes, Managers must create new worlds and then destroy them, and then create anew ... such brave acts of creation must begin with a vision that not only inspires, ennobles, empowers, and challenges, but at the same time provokes confidence enough, in the mist of perpetual competitive hurricane, to encourage people to take the day-to-day risks involved in testing and adapting and extending the vision (p. 482).

Matusek (1997) points out that "Leaders should think of themselves as individuals surrounded by mirrors of many kinds" (p.17). Senge (1990) encourages leaders to work with, not against or at the expense of the employees who can lead the organization to increase competitiveness.

Other leadership concepts and theories are based on other factors such as ability to lead, communicate and resolve problems. Leading effectively requires a complete analysis and understanding of the four factors of leadership: the led, the leader, the situation, and communication (Carney, 1999). The intellectual functions of leaders have often been neglected in discussions of leadership. Hesselbein et al. (1996) write, "Force of personality or interpersonal skills have often been stressed more than the brainpower required for leaders to think through problems and find new solutions" (p. 97).

Future Aspects

One can consider the degree of complexity that is being envisioned for the leaders of the future. Drucker (1999) writes, "Large organizations will have to be managed as if they were small, they will have to be both global and local, and they will need to promote both internal conflict and overall coherence" (p. 73). Spencer (1998) writes, "It's virtually impossible to imagine how a single person, in the form of the Chief Executive Office (CEO), could possess the staggering combination of leadership skills, managerial talent, and technical knowledge required to meet assorted strategic and organizational challenges" (p. 34). Drucker (1999) writes, The successful organization of the future will also develop exceptional skills to innovate in two other areas: strategy development and organization design ... if the most critical characteristic of the new business environment is the accelerating pace of change, then the ability to quickly and creatively develop and implement new strategies and the organization designs required to make them work will become a major source of competitive differentiation (p. 73).

Hesselbein, Goldsmith and Beckhard (1996) write, "Tomorrow's work will place even more of a premium on leaders with education and skills" (p.101). Because the new technology is flexible, the organization of the future will see a substantial increase in the number of leaders and workers who work from their homes or some location other than the organization's office. The need for skilled leaders will be reinforced by continuing changes in how companies and other organizations operate, such as use of teams and increased worker autonomy. Kuhnert and Lewis (1987) point out, "Key behaviors of successful leaders may include articulating goals, building an image, demonstrating confidence, and arousing motivation" (p. 650). Leaders of the future will place increasing value on workers who not only can operate the tools of tomorrow, but who also can find ways to increase their company's productivity and earnings. Peters (1994) argues, "With global communication and the exponential rate of development, leaders and managers should embrace abandonment of standard procedures, abandonment of hierarchical chains, abandonment of the norm and unleashing imagination and creativity" (p. 5).

Weiner (1950), who perhaps more than any other human being was in a position to clearly perceive the long-term consequences of the new automation technologies, warned of the dangers of widespread and permanent technological unemployment. Weiner (1950) writes, "If these changes in the demand for labor come upon us in a haphazard and ill-organized way, we may well be in for the greatest period of unemployment we have yet seen" (p. 84).

Drucker (1993) warns his business colleagues that "the critical social challenge facing the emergent information society is to prevent a new class conflict between the two dominant groups in the post-capitalist society: knowledge workers and service workers" (p. 27).

The new information technology of the future will allow companies to collapse layers of management and place more control in the hands of knowledgeable workers and work teams at the point of production. Some critics, like German social scientist Dohse (1985) contend, "Japanese lean production is simply the practice of the organizational principles of Fordism under conditions in which management prerogatives are largely unlimited" (pp. 115-146).

Technology itself creates needs and requires workers to learn new equipment and operations. The 21st-century workers will be a diverse group united by their use of state-of-the-art information technology to identify, process and solve problems in the workplace. Drucker (1999) writes, "Workers will be the creators, manipulators and purveyors of the stream of information that makes up the post-industrial, post-service global economy" (p. 73).

In order to increase strategic clock speed, organizations and leaders will face some challenges ... senior leaders will need a much deeper understanding of the quickening cycle times in their industries ... they will have to alter their assumptions about large-scale change, in terms of the both frequency and speed of major change initiatives (Foster, 1986). Future leaders of complex organizations should enter their jobs with the expectation that they might well be required to reinvent their organizations three, four, or even more times over the course of their tenure. Drucker (1999) writes, "Companies will need to redesign their organizational architectures in ways that encourage the capacity to act in response to indications of environmental change" (p. 73).

The growing demand for speed in every facet of the business will require organizations to fashion the formal structures, processes, and roles as well as the informal operating environment necessary to encourage managers throughout the enterprise to act swiftly and independently (Galbraith, 1973). Nadler and Tushman (1998) write, "The future challenges will be to devise a streamlined process, employing modular design that still retains some of the important benefits - the learning, insight, team building and ownership - that we attempt to create through the customized design approach" (p. 3).

Other challenges for future leaders will be to determine when, how, and in what situations to make the top team more inclusive rather than less. Drucker (1999) writes, "To succeed, organizations will have to develop a competency in the design and leadership of executive teams, and utilization of new technologies, a collective skill that will be just as important as the ability to design innovative strategies and organizational architectures" (p. 73). The most important challenge for the future leaders are to put back the workers to work and make room so workers will stay with leaders for many years (Rifkin, 1995). The new information and telecommunication technologies are also making organizations less relevant as centers of operations. Portable fax machines, modems and wireless laptop computers allow work to be conducted either on location or from home.

Wireless technology will change the way employees work in the years ahead. A recent article by Crockett (2001) in Business Week mentions, "Over the next few years, a variety of new technologies that blend the mobility of cellular with the rich information of the Net will make their way into the mainstream" (p. 150). Lloyd (2001) writes, "Because of the Internet and the speed at which companies can access information and make decisions, change in business occurs more rapidly" (p. 33).

In sum, new flexibility in tomorrow's organization will present a number of opportunities and challenges for leaders. Telecommuting and flex-place programs will reduce commuting time, create more family time, and allow workers to live in areas far from their employers' offices. Kotter (1996) writes, "The typical twentieth-century organization has not operated well in a rapidly changing environment ... structure, systems, practices and culture have often been more of a drag on change than a facilitator" (p. 161).

Tomorrow's leaders will be expected to excel their capabilities in dealing with globalization, constant change and a revolution in information technology. Hesselbein, Goldsmith and Beckhard (1996) conclude, "This is not to say that the past holds no leadership lessons ... indeed, the future will require a wider, more inclusive lens ... we should be speaking not in terms of either or but both ... after all, the future does not lie in either communications or computers but both ... it would not be shaped by either domestic or global trends but both ... it would not be fueled by either established world leaders or upstart entrepreneurs but both" (p. 262).

Conclusion

Most of the safety literature and research studies suggest a dependency relationship between safety incentives, management involvement and employee's attitude toward safety procedures. These sources say management could optimize total expenditures on safety and accident rates by observing these relationships. Safety management was considered a primary indicator of safety performance. Safety incentives are considered a better tool to motivate employees in safety.

It is difficult to change human nature, so let us accept men as we find them and try to prevent accidents by changing the work situation (Kletz, 1989). Jensen and Hodson (1999) write, "Authorities must expand OSHA's and NIOSH's proven interventions to all workplaces in the country ... the more companies take advantage of the

interventions identified by OSHA and NIOSH, the greater
the impact on reducing workplace injury" (p. 6).

Implementing a systematic approach to workplace
safety will require a cultural change in many organizations,
among regulators and within the safety profession. All
organizations need to nurture a "safety culture". Company
policy and workplace practice must dictate that safety
should never take a back seat to other interests. Markus
(1990) writes, "No one should be asked and no one should
tolerate a potentially disabling or life threatening risk in the
name of cost cutting, productivity or any other priority"
(pp. 14-16).

Safety and health considerations must be an integral
part of the operating policies of every organization. The
consequences are too expensive when safety and health are
relegated to a position of just one of many changing

priorities. Major factors that affect safety are considered in relation to the criteria of leadership, strategic planning, customer focus, information and analysis, process management, incentives, employee attitudes, human resource issues and business results (Warrack and Sinha, 1999).

The correlation between quality and safety is captured by Krause (1994), who states "While quality improvement methods strive to minimize the variability inherent in product qualities, safety management minimizes the chance of occurrence, the frequency and the severity of those non-planned events or incidents that can cause harm to workers" (pp. 51-55). Management must have systems in place to collect data and information on safety and health performance. The leading indicators are the safety data that direct management's attention to areas of potential future problems (Warrack, 1999). Safety and health audits are one method of developing leading data on areas requiring attention ... if conducted by third parties, they can be powerful tools in support of improving safety and health performance (Warrack, 1999).

In sum, there are several key research findings regarding the presentation of safety in the workplace, which may influence its effectiveness. First, it is advisable to utilize the theories of social influence by modeling appropriate safety behavior. Second, it is also desirable to give examples of inappropriate safety behavior. Finally, it is necessary to determine the user's previous level of safety experience and familiarity with the hazard. As it was written by Godfrey (1983), "Those employees who are more familiar with protective and hazardous materials require a different approach to safety and safety information that those with no familiarity" (pp. 950-954).

References

Arkin, A. (1996). Safer workplaces are no accident. People
Management Journal. V2, n15. P. 37(2).

Atkinson, D. R. and Court, H. R. (1998). The new
economic index: understanding america's economic
transformation. Washington, D.C.: The Progressive Policy
Institute, 9-19.

Avery, J. D. (1985). An examination of power at the senior
executive level and how it influences the decision making
process in a federal agency. Los Angeles, CA: University of
Southern California.

Ballenger, R. (1995). Government rules on safety and
health.

Barley, V. (1999). Creating strategy. New York: Harper
Collins, 40.

Barr, P. (2001). Smithfield manufacturer of personal
protection equipment. Providence Business News, March
19, v15 i48 p4B.

Blanchard, K. (1993). Raving fans. New York, NY: William
Morrow.

Boggs, C. K. (1995). Increase safety and productivity.
Industrial Engineering Journal. V 27, n 4. P. 38(3).

Brauer, R. L. (1990). Safety and health for engineers. New
York, NY: Van Nostrand Reinhold

Braun, C. C., Holt, R. S., and Silver, N. C. (1995). Adding
consequence information to product instruction: Changes
in hazard perceptions. In Proceedings of the Human
Factors and Ergonomics Society. San Diego, CA. 346-350.

Bridges, W. (1994). Job shift: How to prosper in a
workplace without jobs. Reading Mass: Perseus Books, 14,
67-73.

Brod, C. (1984). Techno-stress: The human cost of the

computer revolution. Reading, MA: Addision-Wesley Publications. P. 43.

Buckman, E. S. (1991). Motivating and retaining people. Executive Excellence, 19.

Carney, P. M. (1999). The human side of organizational change: Evolution, adaptation and emotional intelligence, a formula for success. Widerner University.

Chissick, S. S. and Derricott, R. (1981). Occupational health and safety management. New York, NY: John Wiley & Sons.

Covaleski, J. (1996). The value of workplace safety: Workplace safety is being embraced thoughtful companies. A.M. Best Company Press.

Cowdrick, E. (1927). The new economic gospel of consumption. Industrial management, 208.

Cranch, E. (1991). Corporate classroom. Journal of Engineering Education 12 (3), 237-252.

Crockett, O. R. (2001). Wireless work: The tech challenge. Business Week, 150.

Davidow, W. & Malone, M. (1992). The virtual corporation: Restructuring and revitalizing the corporation for the 21st century. New York: HarperCollins, 126.

Dejoy, D. M. (1989). Consumer product warnings: Review and analysis of effectiveness research. In Proceedings of the Human Factors Society. Santa Monica, CA: The Human Factors Society, 936-939.

DeSimone, L.R. and Harris, M.D. (1998). Human resource development. 2nd ed., Orlando, FL: Dryden Press.

Dial, C. (1992). Incident-focused managers. Professional Safety Journal, Vol. 37, No. 4, pp. 37-45.

Dohse, K., Jurgerns, U. & Malsch, T. (1985). From fordism to toyotism: The social organization of the labor process in the japanese automobile industry. Politics and Society 14, 32, 115-146.

Drucker, P. (1993). Post-capitalist society. New York: Harper Collins, 12-27.

Drucker, P. (1999). Management challenges for the 21st Century. Harper Business . New York, 73.

Duff, A. R., Phillips, S. Cooper, P, and Robertson, N. (1994). Improving safety by the modification behavior. Construction Management and Economics, Vol. 12, pp. 67-78.

Dunlop, T. J. (1994). The vast new labor beat: Reconfiguration of workplace issues offers opportunities for media to expand its coverage. Nieman Reports. Harvard University Press.

Eckhardt, R. (1993). Coordinating regulatory compliance programs. Professional Safety Journal, Vol. 38, No. 11, pp. 16-20.

Everett, G. J. and Abdelhamid, S. T. (2000). Identifying root causes of construction accidents. Journal of Construction Engineering and Management. V 126. P. 52(9).

Feeney, A. (2000). Safety at the workplace. Professional Safety Journal

Fiedler, F. E. (1964). A contingency model of leadership effectiveness. In L. Berkowitz (Ed.), Advances in experimental social psychology. New York: Academic Press, 149-190.

Fiedler, F. E. (1967). A theory of leadership effectiveness. New York: McGraw-Hill.

Foster, R. N. (1986). Innovation: the attacker's advantage. Summit Books.

Galbraith, J. (1973). Designing complex organizations. Addison-Wesley.

Gallagher, V. A. (1993). Safety of outside contractors. Professional Safety Journal, Vol. 38, No. 1, pp. 29-33.

Gates, B. (2001). Net today. Journal of Microsoft and IT

professionals.

Geller, E. S. (1994). Then principles for achieving a total safety culture. Professional Safety Journal, Vol. 39, No. 9, pp. 18-24.

Geller, E. S. (1995). Safety coaching. Professional Safety Journal, Vol. 40, No. 7, pp. 16-22.

Gibbons, P. T. (1992). Impacts of organizational evolution on leadership roles and behaviors. Human Relations, 45 (1), 1-16.

Gibson, M. V. (1992). Safety training benefits employees on and off the job.

Giustina, J. L. and Danier, E. D. (1989). Quality of work life program through employee motivation. Professional safety Journal, Vol. 34, No. 5, pp. 24-28.

Glen, K. (2000). Worry in the workplace: National poll reveals employee concerns over workplace safety. U. S. News. Washington.

Glen, K. (2001). Workplace safety: Survey by employment law alliance. Washington: U. S. Newswire.

Godfrey, S. S. (1987). A methos for correcting biases in risk perception. In Proceedings of the Human Factors Sociaety. Santa Monica, CA: Human Factor, 484-487.

Godfrey, S. S. and Laughery, K. R. (1983). Warning messages: Will the consumer bother to look. Santa Monica, CA: The Human Factors Society, 950-954.

Goldhaber, G. M. and deTurck, M. A. (1988). Effects of cosumer's familiarity with a product on attention to an compliance with warnings. Journal of Products Liability, 11, 29-37.

Gordon, S. E. (1994). Systematic program design: Maximizing effectiveness and minimizing liability. Englewood Cliffs, NJ: Prentice-Hall.

Gregg, G. (1995). Protecting workers to hindering business. Safety Journal.

Hammer, W. (1989). Occupational safety management and engineering. Englewood Cliffs, NJ: Prentice-Hall.

Harner, R. E. (1983). Safety is a duty of management, labor and government. Professional Safety Journal, Vol. 28, No. 11, pp. 13-15.

Harris, W. (1998). Information channel source selection as a correlate of technical uncertainty in a research and development organization. IEEE Transactions on Engineering Management, 23, 163-167.

Healy, P. (2001). Increasing workplace safety boosts revenues. Providence Business Journal. V15, i48. P. 48.

Heinrich, H. W. (1959). Industrial accident prevention: A scientific approach, (4t^h Edition). New York: McGraw-Hill Book Company.

Herman, M. A. (1999). Future work: Trends and challenges for the work in the 21st century. Harvard Press, 209.

Hesselbein, F., Goldsmith, M., & Beckhard, R. (1996). The leader of the future. San Francisco: Jossey-Bass Publisher.

Hidley, J. H. and Krause, T. R. (1994). Paradigm shift beyond the failures of attitude based programs. Professional Safety Journal, Vol. 39, No. 10, pp. 28-32.

Hinze, J., Bren, D. and Piepho, N. (1995). Experience modification rating as measure of safety performance. Journal of Construction Engineering and Management, Vol. 121, No. 4, pp. 455-458.

Hoffman, A. D. and Stetzer, A. (1996). What causes accidents. Monthly Labor Journal, Vol. 119, n12. P. 84.

House, J. R. (1971). A path-goal theory of leader effectiveness. Administrative Science Quarterly, 16. PP. 321-329.

Information Week (2001). It leadership put to the test. By McGee, K. M., P. 30.

Jackson, F. (1981). The implications of health and safety legislation in the maintenance of building. In Chissick, S.S.

& Derricot, R. (Eds.) Occupational health and safety management. New York, NY: John Wiley & Sons.

Jago, A. G. (1982). Leadership: Perspectives in theory and research. Management Science, 22, 315-336.

Jannadi, M. O. and Assaf, S. (1994). Assessment of construction project safety: Symposium of Safety in Building and Prevention from fires. Dammam University.

Jenkins, J. A. (1990). Self-directed work force promotes safety. HR Magazine, 35(2), 54-56.

Jensen, G. & Hodson, R. (1999). Employee crimes. Work and Occupations Journal. Feb 99, Vol. 26, Issue 1, P. 6.

Johnson, S. (1988). Management accountability for safety performance. Professional Safety Journal, Vol. 33, No. 6, pp. 23-26.

Jones, G. (1995). Environmental Information for the Graphics Arts Technical Foundation. Pittsburgh.

Judy, W. R. and D'Amico, J. (1997). Workforce 2020. Indianapolis, Indiana: Hudson Institute Inc., 17-18.

Kibert, C. J. and Richard, J. C. (1995). Integrating safety and environmental regulation of construction industry. Journal of Construction Engineering and Management, Vol. 121, No. 1, pp. 95-99.

Kimmerling, G. F. (1985). Warning: Workers at risk, train effective. Training and Development Journal, 39(40, 50-55.

Kletz, T. (1989). Poor workplace planning adds to human errors. The Oil Daily, April 13, 1987 pC6(1).

Kotter, P.J. (1996). Leading change. Boston, Massachusetts: Harvard Business School Press, 161.

Kovach, A. K. and Hamilton, G. N. (1997). Labor's efforts sustain workplace safety. Labor Studies Journal. V22, n3. P. 57(17).

Krause, T.R. (1994). Safety and quality: two sides of the same coin. Quality Progress, October, pp. 51-55.

Kuhnert, K. W. & Lewis, P. (1987). Transactional and

transformational leadership: A constructive/development analysis. Academy of management review. Vol. 12, 4, 648-657.

Lasey, R. M. (1994). Managing in an era of workplace violence. Managing Office Technology Journal. V. 39, n 2. P. 27(2).

Lawler, E. E. (1992). Pay and organizational effectiveness: A psychological view. New York: McGraw-Hill.

Leontief, W. (1982). The distribution of work and income. Scientific American, 194-195.

Lloyd, R. (2001). Survival guide to the economic turndown. Fortune Magazine, 33.

Loveman, G. W. & Chris T. (1988). Good jobs or bad jobs: What does the evidence say?. New England Economic Review. January/February, 46-65.

Markus, T. (1990). How to set up a safety incentive. Supervision, 14-16.

Martin, E. G. & Wogalter, M. S. (1991). Risk perception and precautionary intent for common consumer products. Santa Monica, CA: Human Factors Society, 931-935.

Mattila, M., Rantanen, E. and Hyttinen, M. (1994). The quality of work environment, supervision and safety in building construction. Safety Science Journal, Vol. 17, No. 4, pp. 257-268.

Matusek, L. (1997). Finding your voice: Learning to lead anywhere you want to make a difference. San Francisco, CA.: Jossey-Bass.

McCann, B. K. (2000). The value of workplace safety. Performance technology at Liberty Mutual Group, Boston.

McGill, L. D. (1989). Guidelines for compliance. Employment Relations Today, 181-187.

McGregor,, J. B. (1978). Leadership. New York: Harper & Row.

Meister, J. (1994). Corporate quality universities: Lessons in

building a world-class work force. New York: Irwin
Professional Publishers.

Meyer, P. J. and Allen, J. N. (1998). Commitment in the
workplace. Personnel Psychology Journal. Vol. 51, Issue 1,
P. 245.

Mills, V. J. (1999). Resistance to corporate change:
Perceptions of first-level supervisors and customer service
employees. Walden: Walden University.

Monthly Labor Review Journal (1996). What causes
accidents: Industrial safety, workplace performance. V119,
n12. P. 84(1).

Nadler, D. & Tushman, M. (1998). Information processing
as an integrating concept in organization design. The
Academy of Management Review, 3.

Nair, K. (1994). A higher standard of leadership. P. 15.

Noriha, B. N. & Goshal, S. (1997). The differentiated
network. Ossey-Bass

O'Neill, N. (1995). Hazards Materials handling and
standards. Safety Labor Studies Journal.

Palcznski, W. R. (1992). Coping with the crisis: Examining
worker's compensation. Best's Review Property Casualty
Insurance Edition.

Pancucci, D. (1990). Working on thin ice. PC User . Nov
21, n146. P. 30.

Parker, M. & Slaughter, J. (1988). Management by stress.
Technology review. Choosing sides: Unions and the team
concept, 37.

Pelletier, R. B. (1993). Total quality management and
drawbacks of incentive systems. Industrial Management, 4-
6.

Peters, T (1994). The tom peters seminar: Crazy times call
for crazy organizations. New York, NY" Random House,
5.

Peters, T. (1984). In search of excellence: Lessons from

america's best-run companies. New York, NY: Warner Books.

Peters, T. (1987). Thriving on chaos: Handbook for a management revolution. New York, NY: Harper Perennial, 482.

Peterson, D. (1995). Playing it Safe: Occupational safety and health administration rules covering the printing industry. American Printer, p. 28.

Pfeffer, J. (1977). The ambiguity of leadership. Academy of management review, 2 (January), 104.

Platzer, D. M. (1999). Cyberstates 3.0: A state-by-state overview of high technology industry. American Electronic Association.

Rifkin, J. (1995). The end of work: Technology, jobs and your future. New York: Putnam Book, 7-17.

Robinowitz, S. R. and Hager, M. M. (2000). Designing health and safety: Workplace hazard regulation in the united states and canada. Cornell International Law Journal. Cornell University.

Roland, H. E. & Moriarty, B. (1990). System safety engineering and management. New York, NY: John Wiley & Sons.

Rothwell, W. J. (1989). Complying with osha, training and development Journal, 53-54.

Salmons, J. (2000). It's sometimes hard to justify safety programs.

Sanders, M. S. & McCormick, E. J. (1993). Human factors in engineering and design, 7th edition. New York, NY: McGraw-Hill, 675-677.

See U.S.C. [sections] 669(e).

Senge, P. (1990). The fifth discipline: The art and practice of the learning organization. New York: Doubleday.

Sheridan, P. J. (1992). Rewarding safe performance. Occupational Hazards, 74-76.

Slaughter, G. J. and Ghormley, B. (1991). <u>Workplace safety guidelines</u>. Gulf Publishing.

Slovic, P. (1978). The psychology of protective behavior. <u>Journal of Safety Research</u>, 58-68.

Smith, M.J. and Berenger, D.B. (1989). <u>Human factors in occupational injury evaluation and control</u>. In G. Dalvendy (Ed.). Handbook of human factors, New York, NY: John Wiley & Sons, 767-789.

Spencer, J.L. (1998). <u>Executive teams.</u> JosseyBass Publishers: New York, 34.

Stogdill, R. (1981). <u>Leadership abstracts and bibliography</u>. New York: Mac-Millan Free Press.

Swanson, R. A., & Torraco, R. J. (1995<u>). The history of technical training</u>. In L. Kelly (ed.), The ASTD technical and skills training handbook, New York: McGraw-Hill.

Swift, B. (2001). Beyond the osha reversal. <u>Risk Management Journal</u>. V 48, I 5. P. 6.

Thompson, B. L. (1991). OSHA bounces back. <u>Training</u>, 28(1), 45-53.

Topf, M. and Petrino, R. A. (1995). Change in attitude fosters responsibility for safety<u>. Professional Safety Journal</u>, Vol. 40, No. 12, pp. 24-27.

U.S. Department of Commerce (1999). <u>Report on the American workforce.</u> Chapter 2—The Many Facets of Skills.

USA Today (1999). <u>Economic anxiety</u>. Discontinuous Change.

Wardrop, M. R. (2001). <u>National safety council AK steel</u>. New York, New York: Newswire.

Warrack, J. B. and Sinha, N. M. (1999). Integrating safety and quality: Building to achieve excellence in the workplace. <u>Total Quality Management Journal</u>.

Watkins, K. (1996). Of course organizations learn. In R. Roeden (ed.), <u>Workplace leaning: Debating five critical</u>

questions of theory and practice (pp. 89-96). New
directions for adult and continuing education: Vol. 72. San
Francisco: Jossey-Bass.

Weiner, N. (1950). The human use of human beings:
Cybernetics and human beings. Boston: Houghton Mifflin,
84.

White, D. D. & Bednar, A. D. (1986). Organizational
behavior. Understanding and managing people at work.
Newton, Massachusetts: Allyn and Bacon, Inc.

Wilde, G. (1982). The theory of risk homestasis:
Implications for safety and health. Risk analysis, 209-225.

Wogalter, M. S., Allison, S. T. & McKenna (1991). Effects
of cost and social influence on warning compliance,
Human Factors, 31 (2), 133-140.

Young, S. L. (1989). Judgements of hazard, risk and danger:
Do they differ? In Proceedings of the Human Factors.
Santa Monis, CA: Human Factor Society, 503-507.

Zuboff, S. (1988). In the age of the smart machine. New
York: Basic Books.